those
hangovers
and outw
awaythose
drink
those
hangovers.drink
and outwit
awaythose
up
away
text
textoutwithangovers
drink
awayhangovers.drink
those
hangovers
and
awaythose

TEXTS FROM LAST NIGHT

LAUREN LETO & BEN BATOR

Th

a

First published in Great Britain in 2010 by
Square Peg
Random House, 20 Vauxhall Bridge Road,
London SW1V 2SA

www.rbooks.co.uk

Addresses for companies within The Random House Group Limited can be found at:
www.randomhouse.co.uk/offices.htm

The Random House Group Limited Reg. No. 954009

A CIP catalogue record for this book
is available from the British Library

ISBN 9780224086530

The Random House Group Limited supports The Forest Stewardship Council (FSC), the leading international forest certification organisation. All our titles that are printed on Greenpeace approved FSC certified paper carry the FSC logo. Our paper procurement policy can be found at www.rbooks.co.uk/environment

Printed and bound in Germany by GGP Media GmbH
Text design and layout by www.carrstudio.co.uk

Introduction

Textsfromlastnight.com is a website that compiles your wildest and most hilarious texts from the night before and posts them for the world to see. Our website receives over 15,000 texts daily but we post only the two dozen or so funniest ones.

We founded TFLN for reasons that include old flings, law school, repeatedly closing down bars and leaving tabs open, and celebrity sexting scandals such as the recent one involving Ashley Cole.

Before that, we laughed and cried privately and among friends over the mishaps and misfires created by pressing the 'send' button a little too liberally. Those fuzzy memories used to live on in our inboxes until we ran out of room or we hit 'delete'. Now they're immortalised forever.

We have deeply penetrated (heh) our database of more than one million text messages to find the best of the best for your reading pleasure.

Until next time:
drink up, text away and outwit those hangovers.

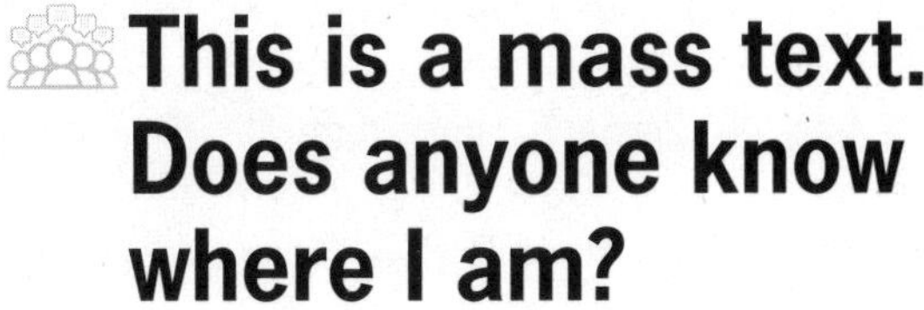

This is a mass text. Does anyone know where I am?

I dont think my parents would of encouraged me to save years of birthday money if they knew what i would eventually spend it on

I would really appreciate it if you would stop texting my girlfriend

I would really appreciate it if you would stop cock blocking me.

My math teacher staples burger king applications to failed tests

I'm giving up shame for lent. Here come the best 40 days and nights of my life.

I just gift wrapped bread.

Just heard a guy discussing with someone else the amazing blow job you gave him. I'm in New York. Over 2 hours away from where you live. I have never been more proud.

>> How to cook rice: 1. put random amount of rice and water in a pot. 2. have sex on the kitchen floor. When you are done having sex the rice is ready

Oh, and bring over your fire extinguisher. We're gonna get the mailman again

Just lost my virginity while listening to rick astley. Torn between horror and jubilation

message sent

You were parading around the bar chugging girls drinks and then asking them if you could buy them a drink. It was actually genius

>> The couple across the street's about to shag. Go get the popcorn and come join us.

Good Times

I'm smoking weed out of a trumpet

I just did a slip and slide down the hallway of my apartment building

Tie

Just got laid for the first time in
3 yrs, 10 mo, 1 wk & 2 days. YESSSS.

This threesome is so guaranteed
that dinner feels like a charade

I just had an epiphany. There is NOTHING TO STOP ME from making cake mix and eating it all instead of making a cake. It feels like my entire life has peaked at this moment.

> You came home covered in oatmeal wearing a tutu holding a stolen rotting pumpkin and 'its a girl' balloons tied around your neck. You were whispering the lyrics to aaron carters 'aarons party'. I think the real question was what DIDNT you drink last night

Only girl at that party wearing a fake beard and I STILL get laid...

I'm pretty sure the new 'vibrating mascara' is just a disguised dildo for those of us who are too ashamed to purchase a real one.

Well, at least their eyelashes will look good while they masturbate shamefully.

Me too. I'd like to spend all next summer high and drunk and riding ponies and boys.

>> I got us presents. Or arrested. We shall see!

Forecast for tonight is alcohol, low standards and poor decisions.

>> Update: Discussing lingerie with my father. He likes sheer black things. Not into the colorful stuff I wear.

Hey you jacked it to warcraft. You can't come back from something like that

He's become way too comfortable around me. He came into the bathroom and took a shit while I was in the shower.

Next time, if you wake and bake, make sure you nail the wake part. Not easy to explain to mum. Or the fire brigade.

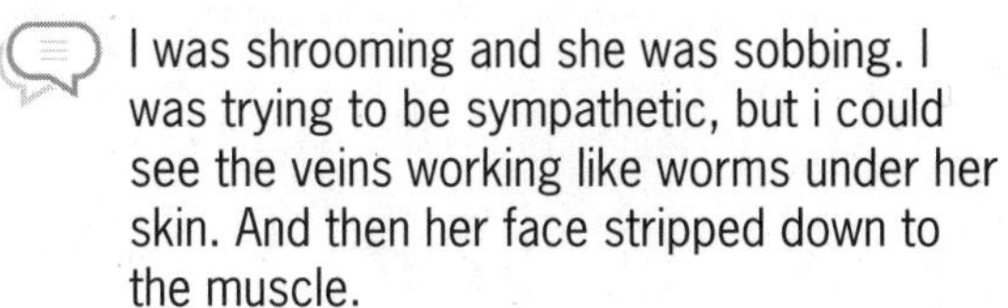

I was shrooming and she was sobbing. I was trying to be sympathetic, but i could see the veins working like worms under her skin. And then her face stripped down to the muscle.

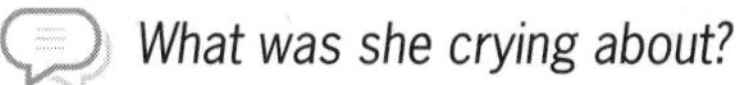

What was she crying about?

I wanna say it was the lack of skin on her face but maybe she lost her job.

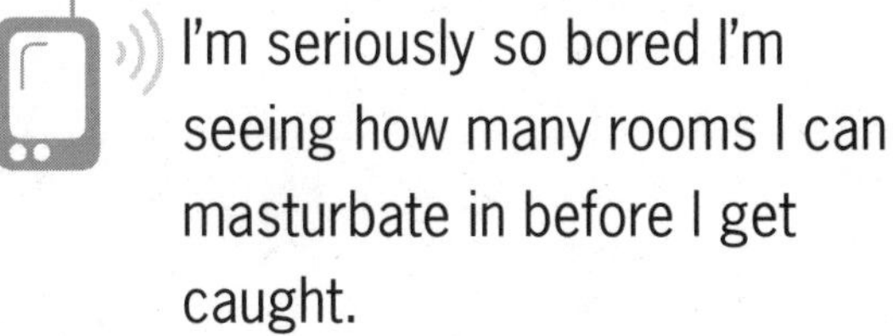

I'm seriously so bored I'm seeing how many rooms I can masturbate in before I get caught.

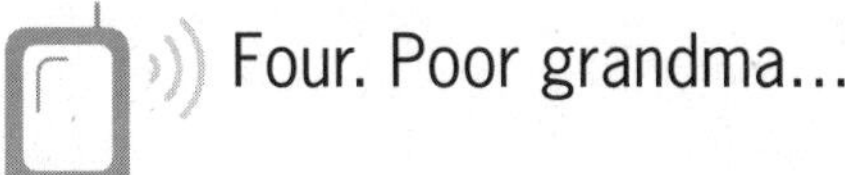

Four. Poor grandma...

I didn't notice until this morning that he had a six inch RAT TAIL...

So he came on my face and then proceeded to say 'that was just how i imagined it would happen'

Where do you find these guys?

I read the police report. You asked the cop if you could use his in-car computer to update your facebook.

Don't worry about later. I already pre-ordered a pizza for a 1:45 delivery and told them to ignore any calls from your number.

You're getting good at this, you know that?

90% of the problems in your life are directly related to your vagina

Puked in the new house. Now it's officially home.

>> I got us kicked out of the bar because the waitress found me in the kitchen trying to make spaghetti.

Before i could say 'i'm not that kind of girl', i was.

I framed a picture of a seagull shitting and hung it in my house. I'm waiting to see how long it takes everyone to notice.

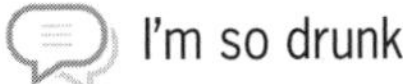
I'm so drunk

Pete, this is bryce's mum

I can't wait to have my cock in your ass

Pete, this is still bryce's mum

He only lasted three minutes, so to spite him i stayed the night and slept in.

The Morning After

If I don't wake up snuggled up to 14 ice cream sandwiches, my life is incomplete.

I just thought you should know I puked up a penny.

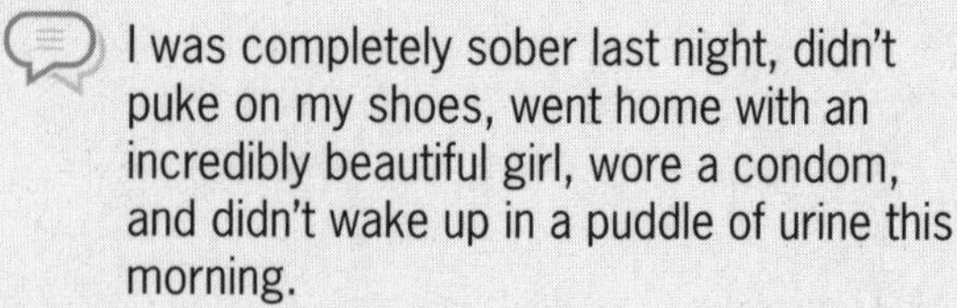

I was completely sober last night, didn't puke on my shoes, went home with an incredibly beautiful girl, wore a condom, and didn't wake up in a puddle of urine this morning.

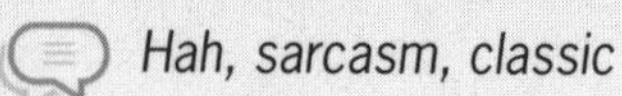

I just woke up in bed with 4 girls. Either i dont remember the best night of my life or they think im gay.

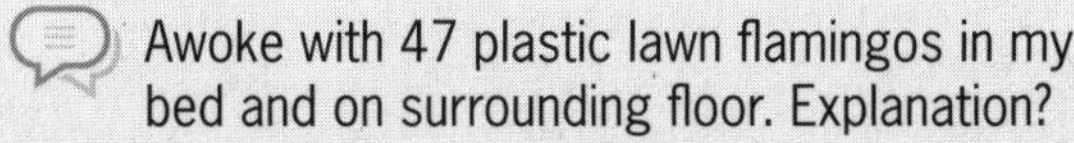

Awoke with 47 plastic lawn flamingos in my bed and on surrounding floor. Explanation?

You said they were your minions of evil that protected you from ferrets.

You left your sweater here the night we had sex and you cried

I've woken up far too early, my hangover isn't even awake yet.

You know its bad when you're praying for a hangover just so you aren't still drunk at work anymore.

I don't quite remember how I made it upstairs last night. Thankfully, the marks trailing up the wall appear to be the mud that I collected from my several visits to the pavement and have captured this journey perfectly

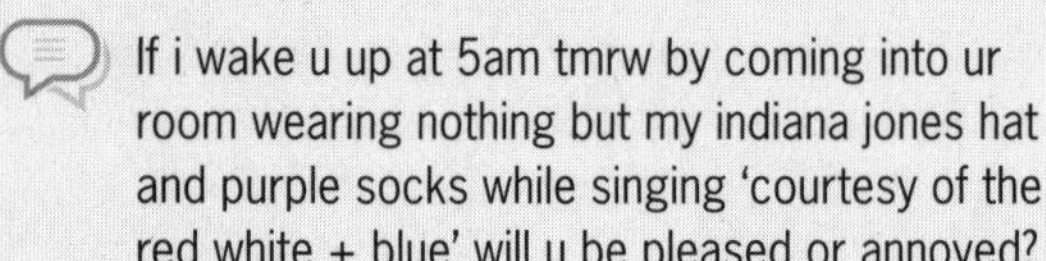

If i wake u up at 5am tmrw by coming into ur room wearing nothing but my indiana jones hat and purple socks while singing 'courtesy of the red white + blue' will u be pleased or annoyed?

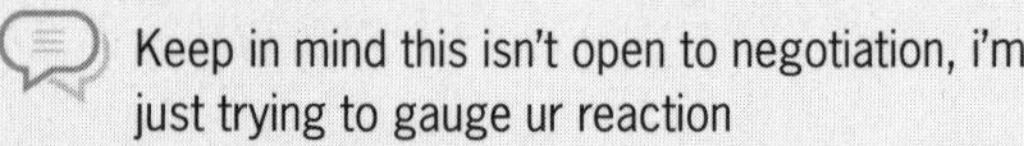

Keep in mind this isn't open to negotiation, i'm just trying to gauge ur reaction

We got drunk. You dropped your phone off a roof and began a relationship with a dog. Id say the night was a success.

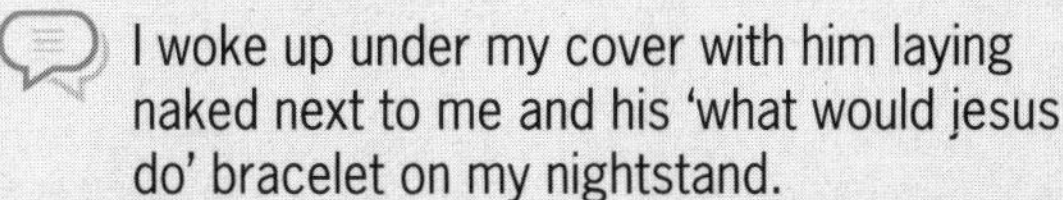

I woke up under my cover with him laying naked next to me and his 'what would jesus do' bracelet on my nightstand.

Nice, that's exactly what jesus would do.

So I woke up in a guy's bed this morning, failed to hook up with him, then went home and masturbated. This is not the kind of independence I planned on celebrating today.

I just woke up surrounded in unopened snacks

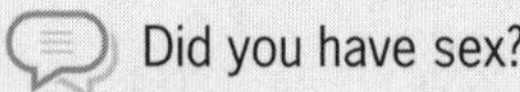

Did you have sex?

Well we both woke up naked and there was a condom wrapper on the floor, but I don't remember so does that count?

Def not…that's how I managed to keep my number under 10 for all of uni – If you don't remember, it didn't happen

How many times do i have to wake up with him next to me, sucking his thumb, before a mistake becomes a habit???

I just woke up with no wallet, no shoes, and a bottle of OJ at the mall. This can't be good.

I'm sorry for everything. I woke up with two citations stapled to my shirt.

I woke up this morning with 'guy in polar bear boxers' written on my stomach along with a phone number…

I just woke up with a girl who has left and right tattooed on her wrists. In french. I may need to stop drinking.

I woke up this morning to the buzzer on my oven going off…I cooked fish sticks at 425 degrees for 5 hours last night. My house smells amazing

3 questions: why do i have a fat lip, why is my bed wet, and why the fuck do i have a plane ticket to bolton?

I woke up to 20 missed calls from you, 3 from a blocked number and had 13 voicemails that all said 'send me a picture of your tits'.

So im guessing thats a no...

Sunday funday is beginning to lead into maybe i should go to meetings Monday

Allegedly i woke up at 5am sat in the dishwasher and peed

I just woke up and realized I puked in my boxers WTF.

You stay classy.

The worst part was I forgot until I tried to put them on.

Just woke up and my boobs have 'fun police' written on them

When I woke up his cat was sleeping on my face and i had scratch marks on my neck. Not happy.

Only room for one pussy in that bed.

Just woke up wearing a top hat and simpsons boxers. I also found more money in my wallet than what i had before going out, about $1000 more

I woke up wearing no shirt sleeping next to a half-eaten cheese toastie.

Well did you call the toastie yet? Or r u waiting the usual 3 days?

I just woke up to a guy kissing me goodbye and leaving for class. I don't know where I am, don't have any clothes on, my underwear is gone, and the shoes I found with my dress aren't mine. He just walked in and gave me my phone. I had my period. Come get me I will walk to the nearest crossroads and wait.

I woke up naked in her front yard…apparently i tried to leave in the middle of the night, forgot my clothes and decided, 'oh heres a nice patch of grass to sleep on'. I think god is up there laughing at me.

I blacked out in 45 minutes and woke up with a missed call from someone I saved in my phone as the karate kid.

I woke up lying next to some guy.
I dont have my bra or his name.
He has a nice tv though.

I threw up in his kitchen sink and then used a measuring cup to drink water because i couldn't find a clean glass. I just threw up down the stairs. It's gonna be a long walk home.

You remember correctly you did get a golf cart ride out but it wasnt because you were special. You were so smashed you were screaming 'Tiger!' at random golfers in the middle of their backswing.

>> You told her you hoped she was a lawyer because she was too ugly to have a 'nice person' job.

The psycho put 'in a relationship bullshit' on facebook...this is not worth it

Watching you get rid of this one shall be very entertaining...

He told me that by having sex with him it would be helping out his marriage.

It was a great night, didn't pay for anything

The best nights you never pay for, except in dignity

I wish i could make my toaster dance like they do in the second ghostbusters. But i dont have ectoplasmic goo. Or a toaster.

>> He asked me if i knew what a blumpkin was... i shouldnt have agreed to find out before he told me the definition.

Removable shower head + gerard butler singing 'music of the night' + wine = amazing

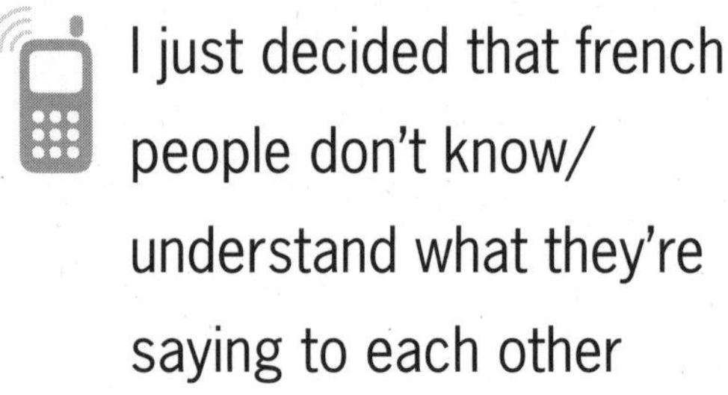

I just decided that french people don't know/ understand what they're saying to each other

>> Yes. At Joey's but he said if you come he'll stab you with the spear in his basement

Rawr!

* *making t-rex arms* *

Sensory Distortion

Smells

I smell stomach acid.

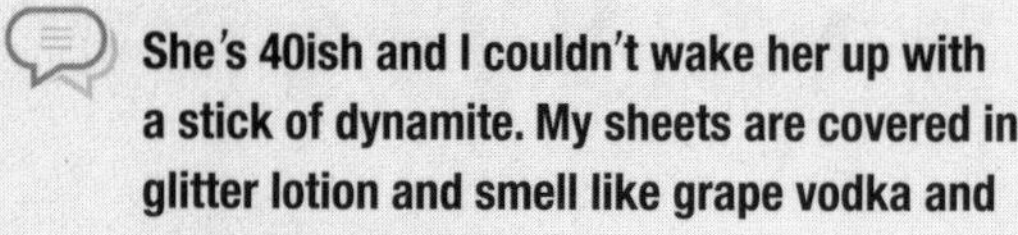

She's 40ish and I couldn't wake her up with a stick of dynamite. My sheets are covered in glitter lotion and smell like grape vodka and shattered dreams.

Aren't divorce parties fun?

You and I have very different definitions of fun.

My hair reeks of homosexuality.

My hands smell like the metro – like jizz and awesome.

Tastes

It tastes like there's a party in my mouth and everyone is throwing up

Im bringing wine tonight. Its a merlot from nashville. I bet it'll taste like infidelity and teenage pregnancy.

My mouth tastes like poor choices

I told him it tasted like his mum... needless to say we were asked to leave.

Jagermeister has never tasted this much like disappointment and horny at once

My mouth tastes like defeat. Did he at least have money?

Drinking non-alcoholic beer is like going down on your cousin.

Sure it tastes the same, but it ain't right.

Looks

My Blind Date Arrived. She looks like something I'd draw with my left hand.

His stupid grin looks like he's mid-ejaculation

He looks like a mix between a retired piano teacher and a cat that just swallowed a sock.

If he looks like a Gremlin DO NOT get him wet.

He looks like Jesus, if Jesus had let himself go.

Smith looks like a guy that goes on a lot of first dates

Not only are you not the girl i fell in love with, but from the looks of it, you ate her

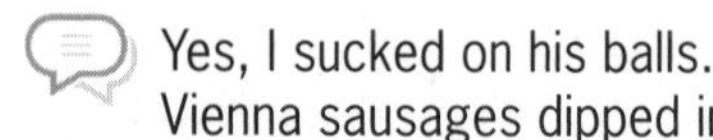

Yes, I sucked on his balls. They tasted like Vienna sausages dipped in tartar sauce.

THIS IS YOUR BROTHER. I am going to need therapy.

And then she said I drew a line on her forehead with my cum and whispered 'Simba'

Our daughter's middle name will be Sangria. Do not attempt to fight me on this.

I can't deal with this right now.

CECELIA SANGRIA IS A BEAUTIFUL NAME.

Do you think people stop being hipsters when they're naked? because that's what my research shows.

You were saying you were peter pan and I was tinkerbell and you had to think happy thoughts, then you put your arms straight out and thought you were actually flying while the cab was moving.

>> I'm in a subway station watching a tranny do her makeup. This is like watching a unicorn giving birth.

I feel like a superhero. Should I use my new boobs for good or for evil?

So I answered the door in my underwear expecting my boyfriend. Instead I opened the door to Jehovah's Witnesses. Do you think that was a sign from God?

Do you think they make care bear costumes for cats?

My phone didn't know the word 'conscience', do you think that is indicative of something?

>> Do you think there's anyone left in this world that hasn't masturbated in a computer chair?

Bar closing I am hiding in the bathroom. Do you think anyone will find me?

Don't you think facebook is a bit pretentious, suggesting friends and all? No, facebook, I would NOT like to be friends with a girl whose fiance I have slept with.

Drinks

Tequila

I dont remember anything after Tequila & Apple Juice. May have discovered the recipe for mental bleach.

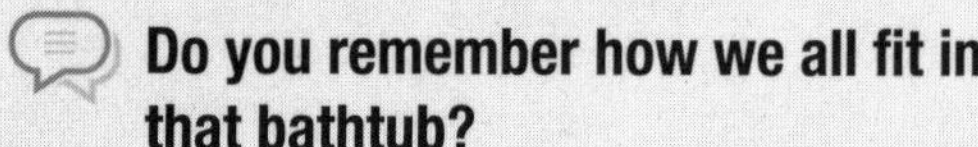

Do you remember how we all fit in that bathtub?

Tequila

I'm chasing tequila w mint flavored ice cream, phil's chasing it w cream cheese, bashar's chasing it w pickles...i think we all know who the winner is...

You decided that the alcohol in your cocktail wasn't enough and had a tequila chaser with everything, water included. You proceeded to tell everyone about your drug habits in front of your whole family. And you emailed photographic cheating evidence to your ex's new gf under the heading 'merry christmas'. Freud would have something to say about how drunk your dad got you last night.

I think tequila should come with a little jiminy cricket

??? When I first met her at the bar, she told me she was 23. After I bought her 3 shots of tequila, she told me she was really only 21. When we went back to my house, she said she was really only 19. She's still sleeping next to me butt naked. I'm afraid if she opens her mouth again I could be looking at 10 years.

It helps if you take a shot of boiling hot tequila right before puking, little trick i learned

Vodka

Mmmm, vodka for breakfast

Fighting downstairs. Join me tonight to hear their makeup sex. Also, let's make skittles vodka.

Hurry and get over. I need a wingman. She is on her 6th vodka shot and her resident ugly friend is still sober

Just took a cab, driver just asked what i'd been drinking – i said vodka, he said 'can't do vodka-drunk, it makes me feel like i'm giving birth to myself'…no comment

Things it involved: vodka, boy parts, possible photos of me on a cell phone. Things it did NOT involve last night: my bra, his pants, and sobriety.

Well for starters i'm drinking vodka out of a red pepper.

Beer

 Wow wtf my bar tab was 80 dollars

 *IT WAS DOLLAR BEER NIGHT*

Why did you take off so early?

No more beer. And also. Threesome. Maybe. Ill let you know.

It's 4 am, i'm drinkin beer and re-drywalling my bathroom. This could possibly be a bad idea.

She said I was really immature but whatever...oh by the way we just bought a toilet and turned it into a beer bong so come over

Everyone should know as good as ramen noodle cooked in beer sounds...its not

Wine

I used a bag of wine as a pillow last night.

We were so bored at work tonight that we were in dry storage taking turns pouring the boxed wine we use for cooking into each other's mouths.
I think I'm starting to understand the 'problem' aspect of 'drinking problem'.

Perhaps when you are drinking red wine from a tall glass with a straw it is time to call it a night.

I'm having a small glass of wine in the hopes that it will revive me. I think my liver just cried a little.

Whatever It Takes

Final count. 18 beers. 4 shots baileys. 2 shots vodka. 1 glass champagne. Vomited in the yard after losing my phone in a field for 8 hours. Possibly played tag with myself

We're chasing vodka with high fives

I'm chasing vodka with french fries.

We're chasing vodka with hard eggnog.

In july?

Do you think if I drink bleach they will let me leave work?

Do you think porn stars masturbate to their own videos?

Do you think fat gay guys titty fuck?

I haven't heard from you in over a month and that's what you come with?

Is it weird that I think of Ennis from Brokeback Mountain every time I hear 'Make 'Em Say Uhh!' by Master P? 'I don't need your money. Huh.' NA NA NA NAAA.

>> All I know is if I don't watch Spice World right now there will be a firefight.

The producers of Marley and Me owe me about $5 million. That's the dollar amount of embarrassment compensation required for making a 24-year-old male cry publicly on an aeroplane while sitting in the middle seat between a gorgeous babe and a guy with a do-rag.

You know the compass Jack Sparrow has? The one that just points at whatever you want? That's pretty much my moral compass.

She's like the female version of the Memento guy. She keeps forgetting that I'm an asshole after we have sex.

I just watched Juno. I kind of wish I was in high school and pregnant

It wasn't awkward until he started humming the Rocky theme song in the middle of fucking

Community service is like 'the breakfast club' ... except we're all the criminals.

>> I tried to gradually lead her into my room but she wouldn't stop crying and quoting Memoirs of a Geisha

Is it a little weird that I have a ridiculous urge to have sex while the theme song to the Pirates of the Caribbean blares in the background?

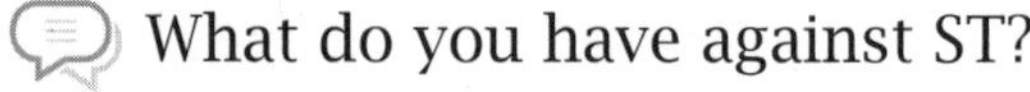
What do you have against ST?

DO NOT ABBREVIATE LIKE YOU AND STAR TREK ARE FRIENDS.

>> I just realized Britney Spears and I are more alike than I thought. Both of us have our parents in complete control of our lives, we both have restraining orders on previous boyfriends, and we all know both of us can put on a hell of a show

I think that we as people have rights and that we should at the very least be warned before being subjected to Fergie

I'm the matthew mcconaughey of this party. I'm too old, and too high.

Cant believe you said you would bone perez hilton

I said paris hilton

Thats even worse

NEED BACKUP we are in the kitchen arguing about who would win in fight against lil Wayne and snoop dogg

>> I'm listening to 'Transmission' by The Tea Party from like '97 and waxing my legs. Fuck i'm awesome in my alone time

>> Someone called me shannen doherty annnd it hurt my feelings

His facebook status quotes britney spears so there is always that

The best thing happened. Some guy was butchering Conway Twitty at karaoke and the power went off in the whole bar. And someone shouted 'you pissed jesus off when you messed with conway!'

Morgan Freeman can narrate your sex life and it still wouldn't interest me.

Weed, chlorine, and victory. My bed smells like i had sex with michael phelps.

It was like a mary poppins bag, except a sexual mary poppins bag.

I just crawled out of a second story window using a sheet and his clothes for a rope so he wouldn't wake up.

I am so glad I watched Macgyver as a kid.

Why did i wake up with a kid named Raphael in my bed this morning?

I dont know but you did call last night to tell me you found the last ninja turtle

Im on my way to getting 'i just graduated with no money, no job, and no plan' drunk

There'll be strippers and coke right?

No strippers. Just coke.

I hate this fucking recession

Please advise as to how precisely ashamed I should be if I just became sexually aroused by a Harry Potter and the Half Blood Prince preview

That Just Happened

Banned from zoo.

Again?

What did we do last night that was yellow?

We just walked into this party and immediately got handed a cheeseburger...

One moment we were outside chatting, the next we all had cowboy hats on and the guy was putting a banana down his pants.

You just walked in and started kissing her, who is she? What did you say to her?

Nothing. I dunno who she is. I think I was trying to say hi and swayed too far forward

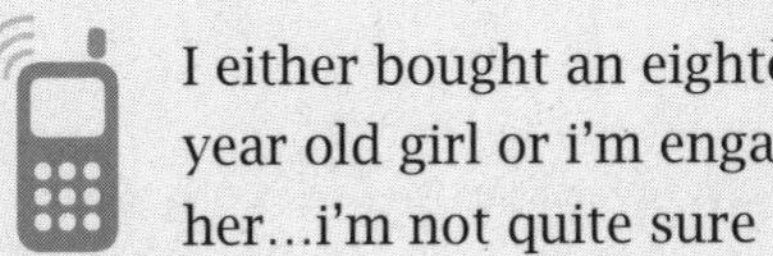

I either bought an eighteen year old girl or i'm engaged to her...i'm not quite sure

All you kept saying last night was how it wasn't morally wrong to have feelings for your cousin. You then proved this by trying to kiss your own cousin. I don't think her dad was very impressed, hence the black eye

My mum just walked in on me furiously masturbating while reading twilight. Needless to say, im officially out of the closet.

>> The police officer looked at my vomit and told me 'milk was a bad choice'

So i woke up to her 8 year old asking for a bowl of cereal...

Woke up naked, spooning with wine bottle...and my video chat was still open. Fuck, not again.

Uni reaches a new low. We just carved a shot glass out of a potato.

Ambulance drove by playing 'What Is Love?' on the loudspeaker. Both driver and passenger were head bobbing.

Drank two beers while on the toilet at home during lunch break. New high or new low, not sure

I think I kinda wanna bone that ginger from Harry Potter.

You literally just made my flesh crawl.

Apparently last night I sat at the bar with an upside down sharpie lightning bolt on my forehead, yelling 'It's Harry Potter's birthday! Let me be on the quidditch team!' And I kept calling the bartender Dobby. There are videos.

And God said, 'Let there be Twilight,' and it was so.

I should injure you considerably.

he is naked. in. my. bed. happiest day. of my. LIFE.

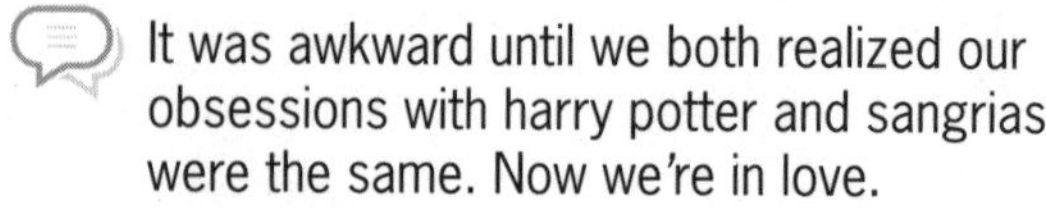

It was awkward until we both realized our obsessions with harry potter and sangrias were the same. Now we're in love.

You need to get a life and stop texting me about fictional characters. I don't give a shit.

Maybe i would like her more if 99% of her sentences didn't start with 'yesterday when i was reading Twilight ...'

It's about making memories worth repressing

You were telling me about how you were gonna marry him, have his children and name them all woodchip.

I'm once again drinking at 8am on a Sunday in my tutu. This garment is literally my best purchase ever.

>> So I don't have any furniture but we just skateboard drunk around the floor.

Don't go all Obama on me. George Bush this decision and just do it. Thinking's for the morning after

Choose Your Own Bad Decisions

Bar or house party tonight

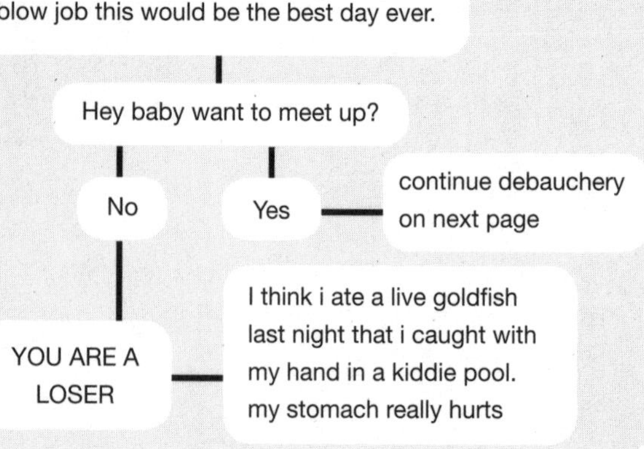

House party
im in a kiddie pool, high, with a keg in arms reach. If I had a sandwich and a blow job this would be the best day ever.
Hey baby want to meet up?
No
Yes
continue debauchery on next page
YOU ARE A LOSER
I think i ate a live goldfish last night that i caught with my hand in a kiddie pool. my stomach really hurts

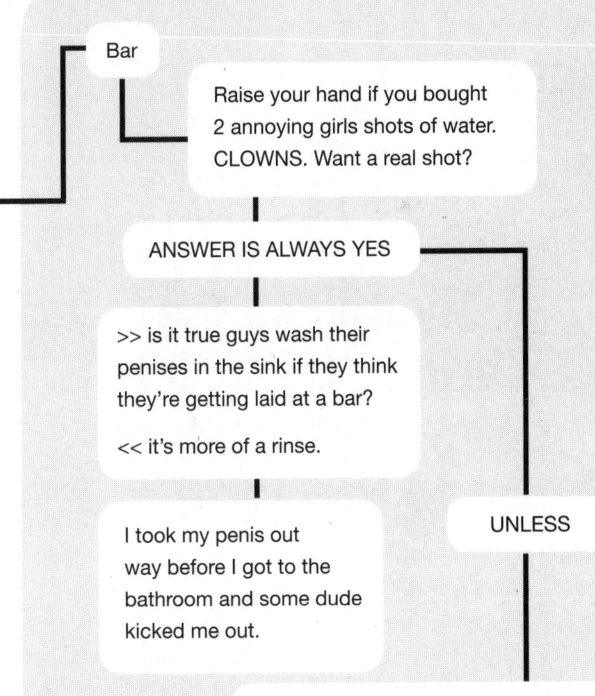
Bar
Raise your hand if you bought 2 annoying girls shots of water. CLOWNS. Want a real shot?
ANSWER IS ALWAYS YES
>> is it true guys wash their penises in the sink if they think they're getting laid at a bar?
<< it's more of a rinse.
I took my penis out way before I got to the bathroom and some dude kicked me out.
UNLESS
I can't take that shot because I want my penis to stay hard.

My milkshake brings 85 to 90 percent of the boys to the yard

I just hatefucked a Bush administration appointee. Now having celebratory mimosas.

>> I told him I hadn't been laid since Bush was president. Right after he cums, he says 'Welcome to the Obama Administration.'

Let's have some freedom sex

I don't love our country that much

You told everyone your name was brenda and you had the whole party chanting b-dawgg by the end of the night. Successful.

Professionals

Just saw a policeman use his lights to go through a red light only to turn them off and pull in to a fast food place.

Apparently smacking a customer in the face with his iPhone was not part of the WOW factor we learned in training...

I just had to pull over at a starbucks to throw up in the bathroom. They really should not have let me be a lawyer.

In retrospect, pretending to punch a 9 year old girl in the face was a terrible analogy to use in a piano lesson.

Philosophical question: how many blocks away from the office do I need to be before I can order a cocktail with lunch? Pls remind me to tell you about my left nipple.

Searching for a job in this recession is like trying to find the clit. I'm screwed

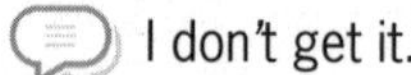
I don't get it.

Me neither.

But I masturbated to it anyway.

It was beautiful and magic like when a hot girl grabs her own tits and smiles at you

I wanna do a homemade sex video in sepia and pretend we're in the early 20th c

I am engaged

To a real live girl that has met me

>> Watching university challenge and taking a shot every time i want to punch one of them in their posh faces. Goodbye sobriety

Acorns are poisonous if you stick them up your bum

Get your tongue out of his mouth, get your hand out of his pants and GO HOME

Let's make love on the newspapers that declare financial doomsday

Fucking love it maybe bedazzle some baby seals? Make them cuter? Who would club a bedazzled baby seal? Only a fucking monster.

Whenever I'm sad I just imagine if babies were born with moustaches...

Why are there goldfish crackers all over my bed?

You decided you wanted to name them & keep them as pets.

Hey this is lauren, i have to type for jon because he's convinced the tongs he's holding are his real hands

>> I have no tv, fridge, heating, shower or sofa, and there are condoms all over the floor, but I found the corkscrew!

Just woke up in a skip and am currently on the highest odds to make a lecture on glaciers ive managed all term. Commitment? I think so

Don't Let These People Near Children

I woke up this morning in a strange bed with a kid with an accent playing with my feet.

There's a woman at Starbucks that keeps pushing her stroller into me.

Punch her baby.

I just sold weed to a guy holding a baby... does this make me a bad person?

Is it wrong to smoke out middle schoolers?

Yes...dear jesus what did you do?

IBwahaha. Ask your little brother in about 20 minutes. Im dropping him off.

When my kids ask how I lost my virginity Im going to have to tell them of a mythical thing called 'Myspace' and how strangers could lure you into their 'den of love' thanks to clever quotes and graphics

I hate you, and I hope you have babies soon that you love very much. Then I will steal them and feed them to sharks, and you will be so heart broken that you never want to have any more kids and you'll just hide out in a dark room all day wondering how someone could feed another persons babies to sharks.

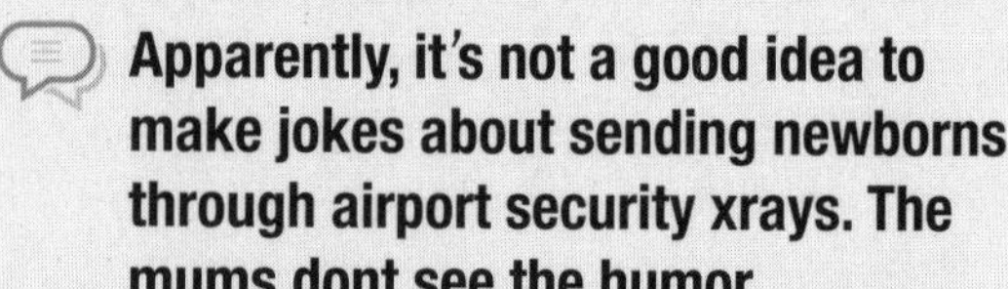

Apparently, it's not a good idea to make jokes about sending newborns through airport security xrays. The mums dont see the humor.

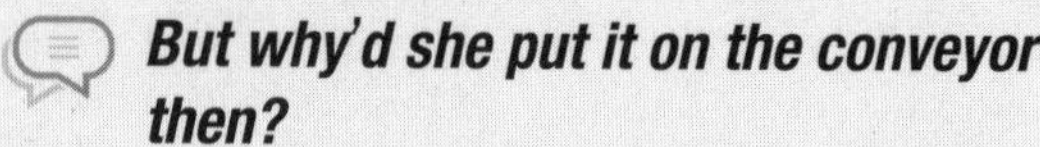

But why'd she put it on the conveyor then?

Sometimes I get depressed that my son is too young to understand how hot his babysitter is.

I wonder what percentage of toys r us merch ultimately becomes a sex toy…

In my case? 100%

Mystery Google just offered me drugs. Damn this thing. I've only written one sentence all day.

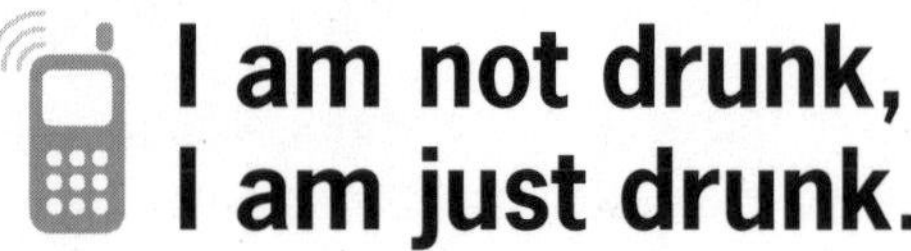
I am not drunk,
I am just drunk.

Oh my god. They have made Journey's 'Don't Stop Believing' into a dance track. Tonight, my innocence was stolen and my dreams died.

I weep a tear for humanity. Is nothing sacred anymore?!

What kind of world do we live in?! I believe in *nothing* anymore...

I think I would 'do' Mayer as long as he sang the whole time.

Which in retrospect would be a little weird.

How's it going over there?

I probably need back surgery and a few organ replacements, but I'm no longer single…

AAARRRGGHH!! yOUR mum gave me SOO MCUUh wine!

They were both wearing bacardi cowboy hats

Totally asking for you to get them confused

I so dont wanna talk about 'what i wanna do with my life or what i like to do for fun' besides drink, i'm trying to get PANTS SHITTING DRUNK here! who the fuck is this buzz kill!?!

I'm watching those videos we made when we were drunk.

Where we thought we were in the blair witch project and ran through some woods screaming? That was fun.

Ugly bird and go home early or keep drinking and have a horrendous hangover, that is the question.

You can have a hangover without an ugly bird next to you but you can't have an ugly bird without a hangover

Munchies

A little girl and i are having a face making battle in mcdonalds

She started it, but I totally finished it.

Is it bad that the cashier at the drive thru shouted 'see you tomorrow!' as i drove away?

I burst into tears in the middle of the mall because I could see starbucks but not get to it. Caffeine addiction anyone?

I feel fat after drinking my meal replacement shake.

I added chocolate sauce, a bag of m&ms and a crushed up brownie to make it taste better.

Assholes at mcdonalds drive thru wouldn't serve us last night even though we said we were on small motorcycles that were too small for them to see and weren't heavy enough for the sensors. We made noises and everything.

3 cheeseburgers, a big bag of doritos and chicken. Hangovers and eating disorders don't mix

Note to self: pasta covered in salt and dipped in ketchup is not a french fry substitute. Still ate it all though

He shouted my World of Warcraft name while we were having sex, and he was sober.

I have no idea, weirdest night EVER. Such a strange conclusion. Why were you naked on webcam to bob's brother? Life continues to amaze me

I'm totally eyefucking that guy across from us

You do realise staring awkwardly at someone until they want to die doesnt qualify as 'eyefucking' right?

I'm gonna be that girl who goes to the bank manager and asks for more money because I spent my student loan on McDonalds and handbags.

And then proceed to sleep with him until he gives it to you

>> Some people speak foreign languages when they're drunk. Apparently I start speaking to Jesus...

Wait mate im serious what do i do if there is pomegranate stuck up my vag?

You announced to the whole party that if she wasnt going to service your needs then you'd give yourself a bj. That's what brought the party to a close. Did you manage it btw?

Send my love to your mother. Probably best to leave out the 'throw your sausage down my hallway' emergency bit out.

I hate average size guys! They are too big to be an easy bj, and too small to be a good lay.

What is better – an easier bj or a good lay?

I never said i knew all the answers of the universe...

Just took twoo tabs
of accidd and am
at cirque de soileil.
Wisssssh me lucckk

All-Time Lows

C what happens when ur not there. I'm still up doing coke sitting in a dog basket.

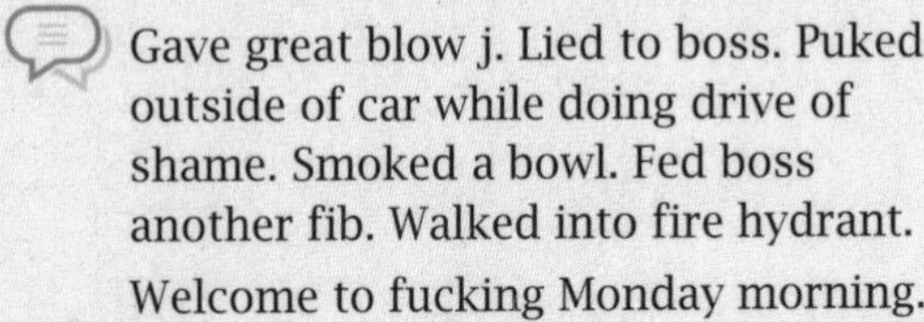

Gave great blow j. Lied to boss. Puked outside of car while doing drive of shame. Smoked a bowl. Fed boss another fib. Walked into fire hydrant. Welcome to fucking Monday morning.

Just wear a hood. You're not obligated to talk to anyone when you have a hood on.

Just rolled into work havent slept still drunk its sunday i dont need to be here

All time low ... just gave a strip tease to the theme song from Law&Order SVU.

Sorry. Sorry. Sorry. Sorry. I love you. Sorry for that, too. Sorry. Sorry. Goodnight.

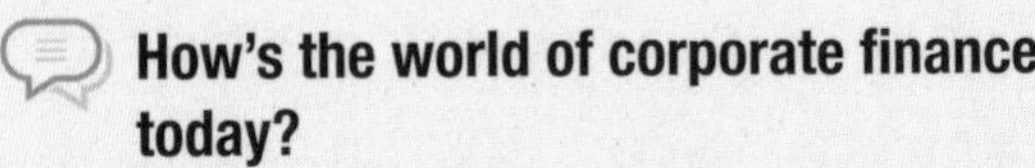

How's the world of corporate finance today?

In a shocking turn of events, people refuse to pay what they owe, threatening letters are sent and I lose the will to live one cup of bitter instant coffee at a time.

The sex was so bad, i'm pretty sure i had an anticlimax

She didn't even bother to pretend she came.

Chris is laundering money. Someone spilt whisky on it, so he is towelling it dry.

We found him lying outside the hotel room wrapped in a blanket with a black eye, crying because he 'didn't deserve a bed'.

>> I have no idea what's going on, but this couch is made of crocodiles.

She said she only went out with me for a week after we hooked up cos she didn't wanna look like a slut. I then told her i was just happy to get 6 more blow jobs

Being in a relationship is amazing. About an hour and a half ago I came home from the supermarket and said 'I bought all the things you need to make me a cake' and kimberley said that I was cute. About 10 minutes ago I ate cake. She's totally not faking her orgasms.

So apparently hair removal cream looks like hair repair cream when im drunk. I also cant come out with you Thursday

The older i get the stranger drugs and men i find inside me

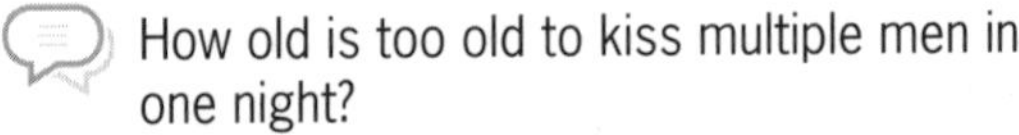

How old is too old to kiss multiple men in one night?

You're about 40 years too late mum

How do you undo a friend request on facebook? I just added her but i think its too soon, we only met today and she saw me go through her phone to find her surname

You just sat up and started talking in like fucking japanese or something

That was me?

He's got too many facebook friends to be a sexual predator

>> Not sure. The last time we saw her she was driving a golf cart into the sea.

Bring booze and girls. Separate, or one already in the other. Your call.

Just heard the extended version of 'I Gotta Feeling' and wanted to commit suicide even harder during those extra 44 seconds

I just need to figure out how to block him in real life

>> Her sex list was a LOT longer than mine. She tried to justify it by saying '4 of those don't count because they were in the gang bang'.

So what's the moral of this story? Aside from 'lesbians hold grudges'?

Caning It

Just figured out how to smoke weed with a toaster.

So the weed I found in my fridge is actually lettuce. Tell jim I need that 5 quid after all

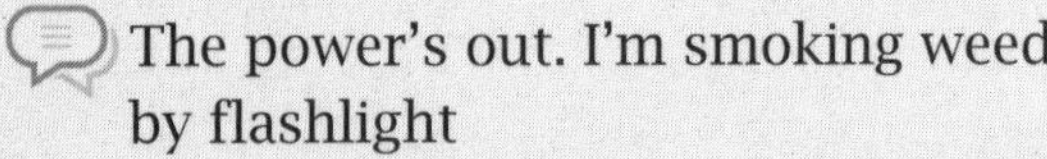

The power's out. I'm smoking weed by flashlight

I wish i was dedicated to anything like you are to weed

I got so high last night I started crying because i couldn't stop thinking about how scary space is

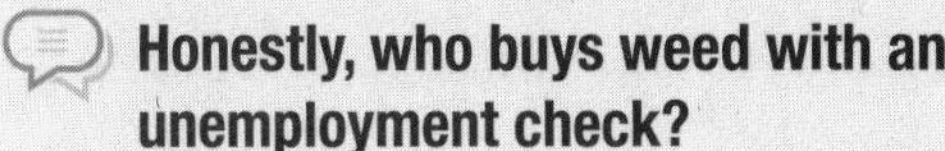

Honestly, who buys weed with an unemployment check?

You.

Oh yeah. Preciate

I'm so high i feel like the people i'm chatting with online can somehow see that i'm naked.

I hate seeing commercials about babies when i'm high

Yeah, I don't like babies at all

I'm inner monologue high

I can totally tell he's high. He's having a conversation with my dog.

So I was just driving high and I stopped to let a pinecone cross the road because I thought it was a hedgehog.

I have a strong urge to join the asians in the park doing tai chi. I think im still high.

So i ate the brownie and i don't feel any high at all. I did however just eat 6 slices of pizza though, which i find amazing…

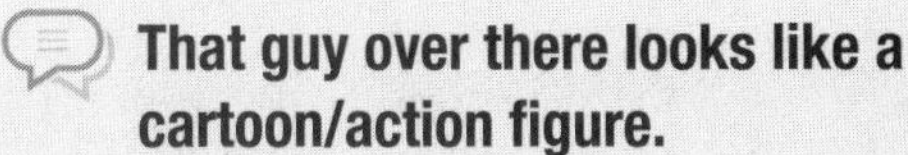

That guy over there looks like a cartoon/action figure.

Omg, i know.

We're too high.

On a scale from 0 to 24…wait, 3 to 24, where 6 is the lowest and 12 is the highest, how freaking high are you right now?

When are you coming home?

When the phone isn't in 3D.

Last night we were drunk and talking about rude things, I mentioned felching and had to explain it to everyone. Everyone was disgusted and asked how I knew about such filth and I told them you told me. Don't get mad. Also a quick heads up, you might get gifts of straws at work.

Having dinner with my dad, watching the news and some AIDS prevention ad comes on. My dad then kindly informs me that he doesn't enjoy the feel of condoms.

Just had to open a tuna can with a spoon. Gave me a sense of hunting for my own food.

She has 2500 facebook friends. I probably should have used a condom.

>> She is my favorite of all the girls you have fucked. Other than me.

I'm half bulimic – I binge but forget to purge

Relationship Timeline

First Meeting –

Hey, we just made out in the backyard. I'm inside now and you should come to the bathroom and meet me.

First Night Together –

He confessed his love for me, threw up on my pillow and then fell asleep on said pillow. I met him last night.

Better than last weekend. Things are really looking up for you.

First Date –

Make note: the first date is too soon to make the 'condoms are only for making balloon animals' joke.

First Fight –

Maybe if you didn't yell 'buh duh duh da duh da dats all folks' when you came she wouldn't have left last night

First Time Meeting the Parents –

I just puked on his mum.

You told him you were too drunk to meet his parents. Totally his fault.

First Breakup –

I accidentally broke up with him while I was drunk which is really too bad since I'd just gotten a birth control prescription so we could start having sex.

Do you think he'd take me back if I said 'hey, we need to get back together or this coil is going to have an existential crisis for not realizing its full potential'?

First Makeup –

But it happened after you broke up with me and before we made up.

First Rebound –

JACOB AND UGLY BROKE UP

First Time Seeing Each Other Again –

It was good seeing you tonight, I'm glad we could be cordial around each other

'Butterface', 'the bitch from hell' and 'crazy fuck' is how our table referred to you. It was great seeing you as well.

This girl is more easily done than said...

You came stumbling down the stairs, pointed at me, and shouted 'YOU DRANK IT! YOU CAN'T UNDRINK IT!!'

Do you remember me telling you, under no circumstances were you to let me go home with the old guy cos I was just letting him hang around to buy drinks?

Vividly...

Then why did I wake up in his bed, dressed in his wife's pyjamas?

I was so drunk last night i ate cereal with a fork.

My brother is at at least 3rd base in the room next to me.

I am in a pub. A man appears to have died in the garden.

>> Yeah lol, and then you projectile vomited on me from the stretcher

Sudden flashback to the works do, me telling 2 colleagues 'what I actually like is girls and drugs' then getting out of the cab and saying 'I know where we are, I had an abortion near here'. Seriously, what is WRONG with me?

I hate the fact that my shower is broken. A shower washes away shame within a few seconds, but with a bath, you have to wallow in it

Gay Pride

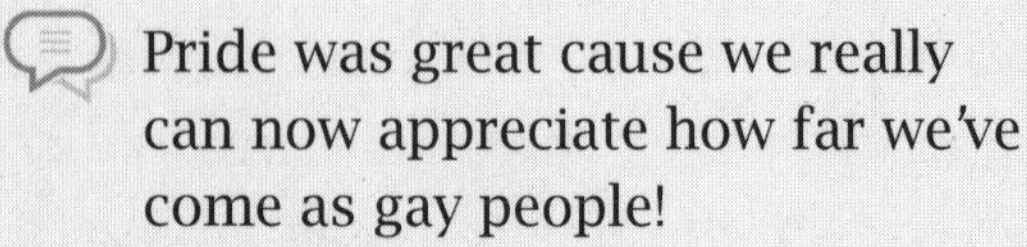

Pride was great cause we really can now appreciate how far we've come as gay people!

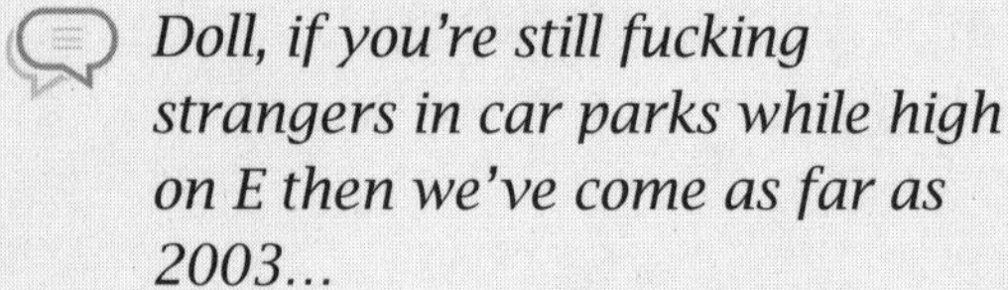

Doll, if you're still fucking strangers in car parks while high on E then we've come as far as 2003…

Woke up next to a guy again. Strike 3 – im officially gay.

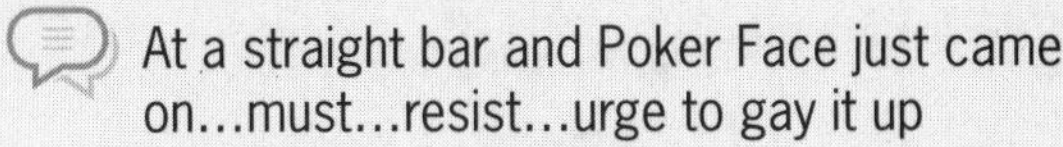

At a straight bar and Poker Face just came on...must...resist...urge to gay it up

Why would that come on at a straight bar? I thought they just played Don't Stop Believin and Wonderwall on repeat

I seem to have left my pride at pride

Gayer than 8 guys blowing 9 guys

Wow, that really makes you stop and think.

You're the unicorn of the gay community. Unbelievable and unattainable.

Mate, I don't think I'll ever be able to find a girl for me…

Is this the gay conversation?

Well I'm going to a gay club in my banana suit. You should come. My bro is going as a pirate. I don't know if there's a theme.

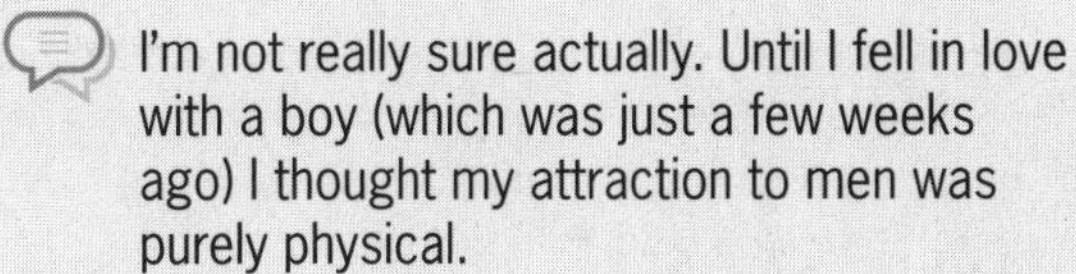

I'm not really sure actually. Until I fell in love with a boy (which was just a few weeks ago) I thought my attraction to men was purely physical.

So you were gay…and then you realized you were EVEN MORE gay

If I don't come home tonight, I've died in a pile of gay.

So its not gay if you have sex with another woman and its academic

So what if I'm having sex with a woman for recreation?

Thats gay

Mate, im on the other side of Leeds accordin to this Polish guy. I woke up in sum1s corridor on an ironing board in a hi-viz jacket. How do you get a train to Headingley with no money? Do you have my jeans? Whos sallopets are these? Answer me these questions three. Thanx fr leavin me btw x

Apparently I fell over in slow motion last night.

It occurs to me that it is very sad that society frowns on drug dealing. It's the one area of modern life where strict etiquette must still be observed for fear of causing offence. Being in a dealer's car is akin to being in a nineteenth century drawing room.

I'm trying to turn this hangover into the best day of my life! I already did the worm in my living room this morning.

>> Mate, she could make a career out of being a 'before' picture.

They weren't boobs. They were lies

I don't think the 'city centre ambassadors' care for their jobs that much, as they've just watched me walk through the lord mayor's flower bed and then piss on a church.

I'm now in a dodgy bar talking to a man about his fatal liver disease while he's smashing pints. Its like I've quantum leaped from the future, to now, just to bitch.

Fifty billion years of natural selection and still something like YOU exists

Oh shit, I totally just remembered about that flying toasters screensaver from like 10 years ago!!

I'm recreating it with all the items in my kitchen. You should be here.

Swapping my gf's and my ex's numbers in my phone. Objectively, very funny. Subjectively, you cock.

Phone Mishaps

Also. You have an iPhone. 'U' is not appropriate.

Renamed my iPhone as 'the titantic' so when I plug it in it says 'the titantic is syncing.'

The iPhone is ruining my ability to sex message. My 5-year-old cousin just picked up my phone at my grandma's birthday party and read 'I wanna stand you up and fuck you from behind' to my entire extended family bc it popped up on my screen

How do you clear previous safari searches on an iPhone? I asked my brother to google something for me and 'big penis' 'empire chinese food' and 'reverse cowgirl' popped up.

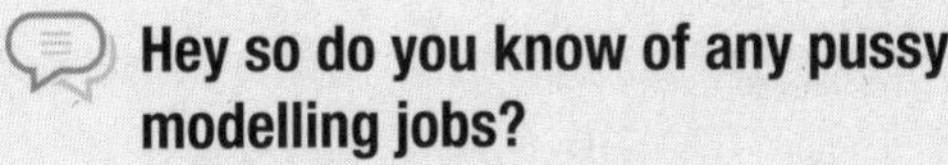

Hey so do you know of any pussy modelling jobs?

PUPPY. I meant puppy sorry

Why do i have 22 missed calls from someone who is literally saved in my phone as bumrape star??

Rather than putting your name in guys phones, you just texted 90999 to donate $10 to Haiti and then gave it back to them

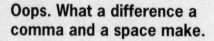

Super hot butfun

Oops. What a difference a comma and a space make.

His sex texting was like a step by step guide to the most boring sex ever...

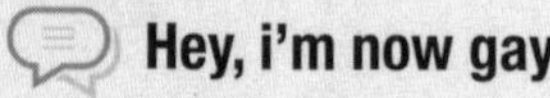

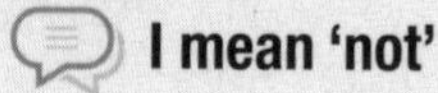

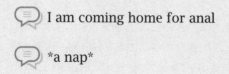

I am coming home for anal

a nap

Seriously iPhone. Stop autocorrecting all my fucks into ducks. You're making all my strong worded texts look harmless and adorable.

My phone writes 'chubies' instead of 'bitches'.

Either way, win, win.

In retrospect, sexting while high was a mistake – I meant to say 'I'll fuck you stupid, baby' but of course I said 'I'll fuck your stupid baby'

I just accidentally send a text meant for you to this girl i was trying to hook up with saying, 'I just got cockblocked by her cousin in the most effective way possible.' Her cousin just died.

Goodnight sugar queer

Sugar queer??

Why does my predictive text prioritize 'queer' over 'puffs'?

>> There is a programme about how bad binge drinking is on bbc. It says that triples in Newcastle are only £2. We're moving to Newcastle.

No, that's not what happened. You were hanging on the bouncer, tearfully begging him to let you in, but you were inside trying to get out.

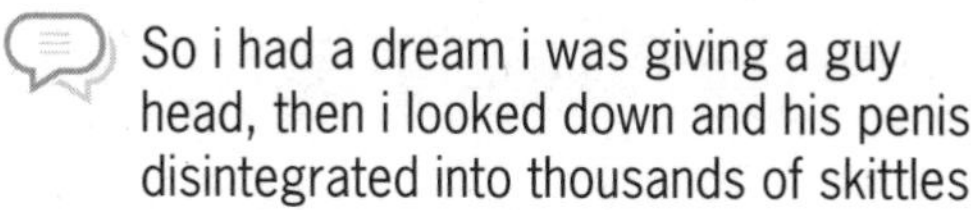

So i had a dream i was giving a guy head, then i looked down and his penis disintegrated into thousands of skittles

I wish that really happened

Sorry, im pretending to text someone else. Dont worry, this plan should result in me getting laid.

He tried. I said no. He said, 'It's ok if I do this?' and proceeded to jerk himself off. Oh, the French.

I'm chasing life with beer.

>> Why are there post-it notes all around the apartment labelled where you guys had sex and in what position?

Someone sent me a drink from across the bar. It was water.

pasta
walking
street
guy

Just saw some guy walking down the street rapping about various types of pasta.

rapping

His dad told me thanks for making his little boy a man at breakfast this morning

I woke up this morning with a bag of pepperonis in my bed...and my facebook status was 'pepperoni'

She's like Mona Lisa when she's intoxicated. No one understands her but they all think she's marvellous

>> Theyre still fighting about whether its called america or the united states.

I woke up to 115 texts from him all saying 'do you love me?'

Texters' Teachings

Tip #47, don't trim the bush when you have the shakes!

Fun fact: cucumber in vinegar with pepper = best ever high snack

Note to self: When getting ready to leave with a kid in a wheelchair don't say: Let's roll

By the grace of god and the ingenuity of Alexander Graham Bell, this text message is made possible: YOU ARE A WHORE

I just walked in on my mum and dad... It wasn't my dad

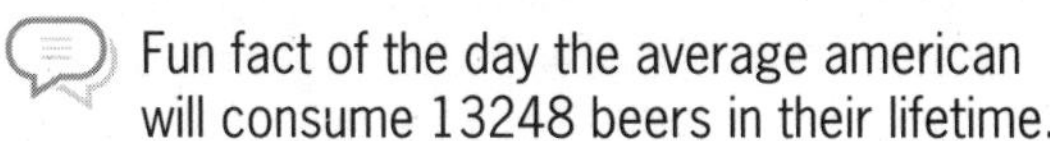

Fun fact of the day the average american will consume 13248 beers in their lifetime.

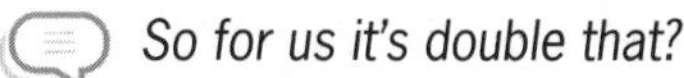

So for us it's double that?

Precisely.

>> So that's a yes to the cocaine usage and a no to the rollerblading

Fantastic night. Drank beer from a wine bottle, danced on a van, chased a llama, and fell from a fence

Sundresses, hats and big glasses. That is the greatest trick the devil ever taught women.

I think I may have given your ex's number to a convicted sex offender.

Win!

Also, i may or may not be wearing a cape right now.

Hint: i am.

I just remembered that last night when we tried to walk off the spins you said 'pretend i'm your pet dinosaur' so i walked you around on an invisible leash while you made t-rex hissing noises.

>> Someone changed all the contacts in my phone to I Like Eggs

Boobs are like coupons for free stuff

Theres bread in your mailbox im going to eat it

Nevermind its newspaper

Tickle wars 95% of the time end in sex.

>> I've decided that life's journeys are more fun when your moral compass hangs in front of you and swings with each step

All we need is a shotglass and a helicopter.

But I don't consider them one night stands. They're auditions.

Life Is Complete

Nailed a girl as she was wearing a darth vader shirt. Cross that one off my list.

I can now get sex on a playground ride off my list of things to do in life.

I just saw a midget ride by on a scooter... wearing a bowtie and a helmet. My life is complete.

Haha so apparently that girl last night thought I was you the whole time, and in the morning realized you weren't the one she fucked. Thanks for your help.

That girl is coming to see me and stay for 2 nights. I'm hitting the 3rd in the trifecta of friends.

You're one hell of a depraved bastard, I'm borderline speechless. You officially win.

They all have matching tattoos so they're all official bffs. I love my life.

I don't know where I am but the food in the fridge is awesome.

Thanks for jumping on that grenade for me last night. You're the best wingman ever

She ate 7 of the 8 slices of pizza. I deserve a purple heart and sex w your sister

The girl i pulled last night woke up this morning, disoriented, and looked at me, and said 'oh, you're hot' and went back to sleep.

I hid a 6pack in the microwave for later

I knew I liked you

When im not freaking out about dying alone and unloved, i actually really enjoy being single

I'm in her bathroom and there's crab shampoo...is it worth the risk?

You're missing what this discovery implies...she's got a fucking bush.

I wish there were wingman of the year awards.

>> **Quick – how do i get carpet marks off my knees in like 5 mins?**

Dating is not our generation's strong point. We're an era that's good at getting laid.

I passed out in Idaho and woke up in Washington vomiting into my roommate's fishbowl. The fish was on the floor.

Don't worry, I took the fish out first.

My favorite part of our friendship is your tits.

I totes stole your whore crown.

With great power comes great responsibility.

Based on who turned up here tonight the whole evening should just be called 'mistakes i made when i was fat'

Where On Earth

Alabama

Only in Alabama do they play hymns in a bar!!!

Arkansas

Arkansas has a gas station called kum and go...story of my life

Australia

R u out the front? Wait there, i'll be out in a minute.

Ok. There's a truck on fire out here. That'll keep me entertained.

Canada

She didn't know my name but she knew I was Canadian so she just called me Canada. It sounded like the national anthem when we were fucking.

Chicago

I just walked outside for a cigarette and three men walked by in glitter heels and gold shiny thongs. God i love chicago

Delaware

At a bar where three women in denim shorts are debating techniques and skillsets for wrangling goats. You stay classy Delaware.

Florida

You're the only person with a favorite bar in Disneyworld

Germany

Germany: the only country where naked girls sit around and play cards. On TV.

Hawaii

How the fuck did we find Hawaii, let alone make it a state?

Idaho

How's Idaho?

Fat.

Indiana

You need anything in Indiana?

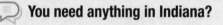

Maybe some meth?

Iowa

I saw a sign that said World's Largest Frying Pan next exit. Way to do your fucking part Iowa.

Ireland

You hooked up with 4 random girls, avoided your girlfriend finding out about it, and dodged traffic on Park Ave. Can you say luck of the Irish?

London

Last night i was assaulted by 3 pairs of drunken breasts and had a girl bluetooth an 'intimate' photo of herself to me. The girl in question is 22, divorced and has 5 kids. Then was offered a BJ by an ex. As a single man i suppose i should be happy, but all that was going through my head was 'the 21st century is FUCKED'. So much for a quiet pint.

Maine

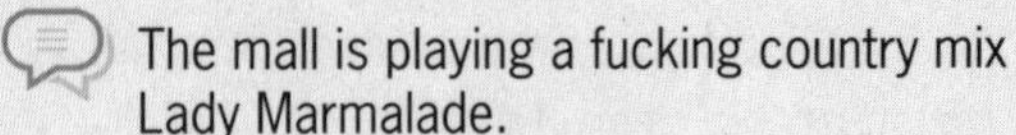

The mall is playing a fucking country mix of Lady Marmalade.

Welcome to maine.

Massachusetts

How is it that boston is so bitchin and the rest of massachusetts sucks so much?

How is it that you still think 'bitchin' is an acceptable term anymore?

Minnesota

The dancing wasn't as good as i thought it would be

Well theyre all white AND from minnesota...I mean they were working with what they had

Mississippi

Just saw a sign on a trailer home that said i'm beautiful, single, and affordable! God i'm going to miss mississippi!

Missouri

Bar tonight had a doorbell to get in and last night i saw my neighbors fuck on the balcony, she wore a nurse outfit. Missouri isn't so bad...

Montana

Only in Montana can you find Septic Services that would display 'Christian owned and operated' on the side of the truck. I'm oddly going to miss this state.

Nebraska

I just saw a man dusting the fake palm trees at the mall

...***welcome to nebraska***

New Jersey

Jersey...The gateway drug of america.

New York

Peeing in bathroom at penn station and the homeless man next to me is combing his beard with a fork...god I love new york

Ohio

Ohio: like a prepubescent girl, flat and unfulfilling.

Oregon

U know ur in oregon when the cop tells u to keep the beer cans he made u pour out so u can recycle them

Pennsylvania

I had to do the walk of shame barefoot on a partially dirt road. I love hooking up in rural pennsylvania.

Rhode Island

In Rhode Island you can strip when you're 16 if you're home by 1130

I love my state.

South Africa

One moment we were outside chatting, the next we all had cowboy hats on and the guy was putting a banana down his pants.

Tennessee

Yeah man, that place is surreal

Man, I'm from Tennessee. What the fuck is surreal?

Texas

Everything is bigger in texas. Including my drinking problem.

Utah

Moving to Utah. Got sick of alcohol and have a severe wife shortage.

Wales

Just went to a pub in Wales – Have never felt so unwelcome in my life – Let's give the country back.

West Virginia

This other lifeguard and I are actually considering paying a kid to shit in the pool

Wyoming

I just saw someone get breathalyzed on horseback...I love Wyoming.

I really love her but I don't think I can go the rest of my life without anal.

Everyone is single if you try hard enough

Just once id like a girl to say to me in the dracula voice, i want...to suck...your dick...

That level of neurosis does not find love outside of Grey's Anatomy.

My cousin's just decided to make a catapult to spread my grandpa's cremated remains. I love my family.

I literally forgot his name and just started calling him 'waffles'

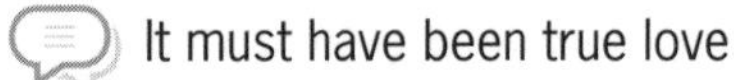

It must have been true love

I don't call true love eating a bag of doritos and then going down on each other

Hey, what's Italian for 'Oh dear, that wasn't supposed to happen yet'? It's pretty urgent

Overheard: 'his girlfriend fucks him with the lights off. It's not serious.'

lmfao. Well really. It's not love if you cringe at the sight of his anus.

I hate this light. I wouldnt even hook up with me in this light

I'm in the sorta mood where i wanna be that crying, drunk girl who will hook up with anyone that tells her she's pretty

>> We were having sex in the bathroom when his aunt knocked on the door

>> And rather than go out and meet her, i climbed out the window. So now she thinks he was masturbating and moaning his own name in a really girly voice

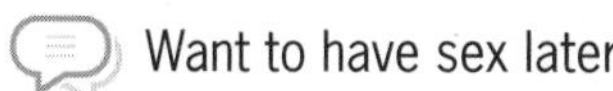

Want to have sex later?

This feels like a trap

Cheats

Im marching my happy ass in there and im not leaving until he cheats on his girlfriend!

Whatever. They have the same name, so it's not even cheating. It's brand loyalty.

U cheatin on me?

If i did i would try to upgrade babe.

The party tonight has no theme but I decided to go as a home wrecker.

This guy asked for my number but didn't have paper to write it down, so he went to write it on his hand i saw he also had the word 'nappies' written.

The red head has a bf

Just because there's a goalie doesn't mean u can't score

My toast was 'here's to being positive, and testing negative ... Cheers!' ... after that chick gagged on her shot, everyone knew ... slut

I either just heard my neighbors having sex or she really agreed with whatever he was talking about.

I just dont know how to see an unattractive person as more than a friend

Thank god random hookups don't end with college. Happy birthday, america.

My goal for the party is to get everyone in a nappy. Reasonable?

She just texted me saying, 'I wish you were a better person so I could fuck you without regrets'

Sometimes i wish i was able to text my cat and tell him i miss him and that i'm thinking about him

I wish mother nature was an actual person cause i'd bitch slap her for sure

I wish you were here to vomit in your hand.

>> I really wish I could go back in time to change the course of events that led to me sitting on the internet at 3 googling 'Traumatic masturbation' while talking to you about failed dates, and running a virtual restaurant in a video game.

Hookup Flowchart

>> Going to meet up with the girl

<< Say my name once during sex just to fuck with her. Like when it gets rough.

Take another shot before he comes over?

if no –

>> How's it going?

<< I'm texting you during a blow job. She thinks I'm looking shit up. Ftw.

if yes –

>> So i completely puked my brains out. A lot. He held me up so i could brush my teeth. Then we proceeded to hook up for the next four hours.

<< He's a keeper

She just waddled down the stairs behind me and puked and kind of reached for me but i sped up. Does that make me a bad person?

I went to disney world today with my friends, met snow white, then saw her later at a bar. She is naked next to me in her bed, passed out. When you wish upon a star...

I just wish we had the ability to download food from our TVs.

>> I wish I could be a nicer person. Or a more sober one.

International walk of shame = epic. Hope there's showers in ireland.

East Village: Only place you can play pac man while eating a pineapple hotdog, go to the bar next door and see a graphic blowjob on every tv

I wish my penis had an off switch

Boys' Night Out

Vegas for my brother's bachelor party. Just landed and I have a boner. I'm giggly and teary eyed I'm so excited.

If I die today, promise to let the world know I partied...oh god did I party

Highlight from tonight: i hit on her and her mother.

Do you remember pissing out the door last night?

Ahh dear, no i dont?

Yeah you said you were marking your territory so that when the delivery guy came, he'd know it was your house. Quite logical in an animalistic way

I knew you were gonna be a good wingman when the words 'dibs on the chunky one' came out of your mouth.

I have to decide between the hot young blonde with no apparent gag reflex, and the brunette with a great ass and a trust fund.

It was at that point the crowd that gathered realized i wasn't getting arrested, and passed the sobriety tests. I got a standing ovation from 25 strangers

I remember going home with 2 girls. Woke up with 4.

We're getting ready to take strippers to breakfast. I love my life.

I just came out of my doctor's office and i look into the window and i see a guy sitting in the front seat getting head.

Why are you so shocked? You live in brooklyn.

Who would have guessed that ordering a vodka lemonade at Roscoe's was code for I want a hand job

I just saw a homeless guy running after a pigeon, catch it and put it in his jacket pocket. I'm not sure if the bird is now his pet or dinner!

I would do things to you that would get us burned at the stake if we lived in a puritan village.

Booty call?

You don't even follow my twitter

Do you think a beautician would be willing to wax the Chanel Cs into my crotch? That way, whenever a guy gets ready to pound on it I can go 'Careful, it's Chanel.'

If only Ben were 51% gay instead of 49%

He puts the penis in happiness.

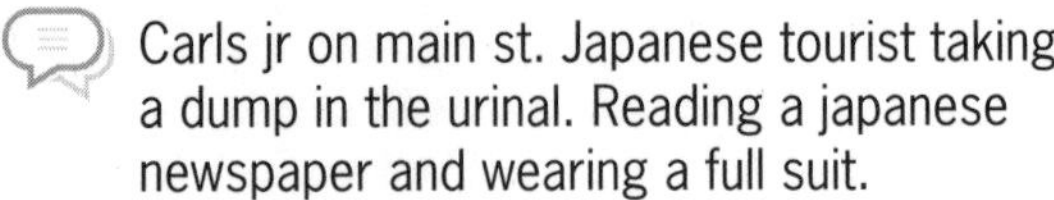

Carls jr on main st. Japanese tourist taking a dump in the urinal. Reading a japanese newspaper and wearing a full suit.

Be there in 3 mins

What do 4 police cars, 1 ambulance, and 2 fire trucks have in common?...My driveway

>> He invited me to an all week drinking party at his house. Apparently he knows the key to my heart is booze shaped.

Im not sure whos apartment i woke up in but i just showered here and their shampoo is phenomenal

Also, you're talking to the girl for whom 'deformed baby arm' wasn't quite a dealbreaker.

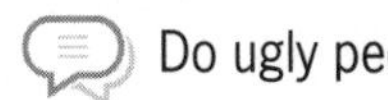

Do ugly people know they are ugly?

The quiet ones do.

I gave her the chance to be interesting and she failed. So then I gave her a chance to be slutty and she failed at that too.

Dear Mark, please dispose of your crusty mcdonalds napkins used to jerk it at my desk

Discreet masturbation is a lost art

I keep telling myself in the mirror 'get undrunk'

I thought I was riding a bike, but I guess it was a vacuum cleaner

We just picked up about 540 lbs of women...

>> Too bad my picture didn't come thru. It was one of me naked riding a unicorn with a wizard hat and a magic staff. And the unicorn had wings. And me too.

Yes, one should always join a cult. At least once.

This is your Morning Wood Report: I have it.

If you're ever in Seattle we should Fuck. Or get coffee, whatever.

The weather is perfect in Seattle right now. Warm enough for girls to not wear bras, but cold enough for me to see them nipping out in the shade.

Don't feel obligated to get back to me but I think I just fell in love with a middle aged waitress in Texas. She's used but in good condition.

Would you ever date a girl who drove an 89 Chrysler LeBaron? – for the record it's a convertible

So I used to make fun of texas a lot, then I got here and I found a place where I could get my tequila in a to go cup with a straw and I realized that this is the only place I ever want to be

Confirm your location. A cross street is best, but if google mapping yourself is your least-shameful option go for it. Ps – going through his mail for an actual address is always an option.

The shirt is mine, the pants are mine, the bra not so much

Ladiessss' Night

I wanted to iron the shorts i'm wearing. But i'm high and lazy. So i'm using my hair straightener. In bed.

Sex on bubble wrap = best decision ever.

I'm sitting next to this guy at the bar. I wrote him a little song in my head it goes 'there is no fucking chance you're getting in my pants' gonna sing it to him after he buys me another drink.

I just met a guy from Australia at the bar. I asked him what it was like down under and he told me if I went home with him he'd let me find out. I love Australians.

I may be the skinniest girl here. I like this crowd.

Wearing these hooker shoes was a mistake

Girls only wine night turned into a sloppy drunk lesbian orgy again

We fucked twice, I went to the bathroom to freshen up, and came back to him playing 'Your Body is a Wonderland' on his guitar naked in my bed.

Proudest moment: just made a guy walk into a parked car with his mouth hanging open cause of the shirt im wearing.

I just walked into a room at this party and someone yelled 'dibs!'...

What's the point in getting all dressed up and going when i'm just gonna throw up on myself by midnight?

Thought so. I woke up and he was playing with my eyeliner. I MAKE GREAT CHOICES.

I've stopped by a kebab shop on my way home – shush not sober

Argh – my predictive text is judging me! What I meant to say is – shish not doner!

Please tell me how I woke up out in the middle of nowhere wearing nothing but a hard hat and a man thong?

Baton twirling is one of his activities on facebook.

Also he is 'an Ohio State grand champion twirler'. You cannot tell me he's straight

Ran into someone who graduated with us while i was paying for booze in coins. I love it when people from my past catch me in my classier moments.

There are two super hot girls lounging outside my apartment...I almost want to tell them theyre sitting where I threw up last night

U should. Its a good ice breaker

I just saw a dog and thought 'Hey! A goat!' Then realized it was a dog. Now I'm sad.

The best things in life are free. Have that freshly fucked look and doing the walk of shame by HIS girlfriend...priceless

I see an opportunity for you to use your nakedness to cure my boredom.

So my grandma sent me a doily for my birthday – don't ask why, I don't know. Anyways I put my bong on it, I think it actually classed up the joint.

Someone wrote that you're a whore in one of the bathroom stalls

I didn't know I was popular enough to be hated. This is awesome

I have nothing to say, just wanted ur phone to vibrate

Haha you were like: 'I don't want to uh pressure you...' as you took your own shirt off

Just went to get groceries. A cashier said she saw me last night. Apparently i carried a broom back from the party and swept the street the whole walk back...and i claimed to be in the cast of Wicked

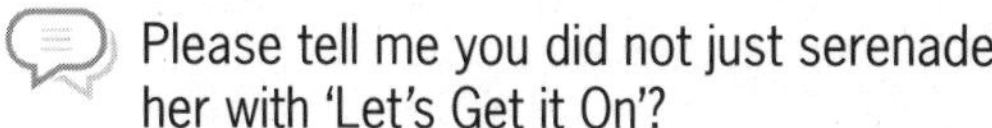

Please tell me you did not just serenade her with 'Let's Get it On'?

Yeah I think it worked. My penis thanks you, Captain Morgan.

>> I think taking a nice shit is a lot more satisfying than an orgasm. This is probably why I'm single.

UNI

On the uni bus doing shots of tequila, salt and lemon and everything. Im on my own. You can feel the jealousy.

Just mixed my johnnie walker with capri sun in a cambridge union mug. Feelin a little like a well-to-do preschooler.

So i'm taking an alcohol survey online to pass a registration stage at uni with glass of vodka in my hand and the first question is 'have you had a drink in the last week?' NO SIR, NO I HAVEN'T.

Porn has gone from 2nd most viewed to 6th since being at uni, proving i've actually been doing work and exploring more diverse areas of the internet. I feel ashamed to be a man right now.

I just feel proud that our time at university didn't just get us a standard degree, we also managed to push a major chain of bookstores into administration.

Out with crowd from uni, totally crazy. I think it's pretty worrying that we're gonna end up as qualified psychiatric nurses – kind of the mental health equivalent of the blind leading the blind?

Woke up this morning to a janitor hitting me in the head with his bucket in the hallway of my building. An alumni was next to me because we locked ourselves out of my room and couldn't figure out where my roommates were.

I need £117 by next week.

Why?

Uni security caught me in dorms doing some stuff I'd rather not mention. There was vodka and a geological hammer involved.

Since i moved back after uni, i don't think my parents like it when I bring a girl back at 4am from a Bar. Sucks to be them

The Ball was amazing! Kinda like a rerun of my year; when i was hammered i pulled fit sam, when i was bored i kissed paul smith, and then i ended up kissing the lad i actually like at the end! Good summary!!

Who on earth is Paul Smith, do i know him?! And the guy you actually like?!

Paul Smith is the guy you kissed as well and the other guy is the one i was texting the other night. Ur coming next yr. it was the best night of my university life thus far.

Grinding on my ninth grade teacher. Dreams really do come true

Before smithy murders me i need you to know 3 things. 1) i got with smithy's little sister last night. 2) i will always love you like my own brother. 3) smithy's little sis digs sex.

You kept singing the copa cabana and saying HAVE A BANANA to random people on the street. You also went up to this poor short guy and hugged him while proceeding to yell I LOVE YOU CHILD MAN into his face. Please tell me you're sober now

Answer the phone when I call you in a second. Just got pulled over for getting road head, going to secretly put you on speaker phone, this should be good

Would you consider dating someone with braces an investment?

Are they still out there making out on the couch? How can we get them to leave?

I'm gonna go stand naked in the kitchen with a knife

>> Fat strippers do more and I don't care who knows it.

So it turns out she's 40 and has a 20yo daughter.

Do you still want to do her?

I'd rather nail her daughter now.

Lets give the
barman the bail money
in case they lock us both
up for this.

Woke up next to a random this morning, pointed and said 'stranger danger', he did not find it funny

I woke up today, looked in the mirror, and said 'Today, I don't give a fuck who sees my penis.'

Memory from last night that just came back: me forcibly jacking him off while he yelled I DONT LIKE HANDJOBS I DONT LIKE HANDJOBS

He kept trying to stuff the yorkshire terrier in his mouth. Poor thing looked terrified.

I think we should go ahead and pin a note to my shirt when we go out that says 'do NOT buy me shots'

On the back we can put possible side effects may include: indiscriminate making out, brief crying spells, yelling in jibberish, and sudden sleep.

I'm at a crab and wine festival with my dad. He just introduced me as his girlfriend to all of his co-workers. I am so drunk I thought he was serious.

>> Don't be mad at me. I know peeing in your drawer is 1 thing and peeing on you while you're sleeping is another, but im sorry... i love you

I'm glad you talked me out of that flying penis tattoo.

Omg. Weirdness. This guy just followed me 5 miles in a car to ask for my phone number. I think he would've gone farther but i pulled over and asked him what the fuck he was doing.

Well did you give him your number?

Haha yeah. I mean he worked so hard for it...

>> I think god invented the sun to punish me when i drink too much.

I am whisper screaming to bohemian rhapsody in my cubicle...but I have no booze for the epic part so I chugged my coffee...not as epic

Agreed. Platonic mermen only.

I dont think mermen have penises anyway where would it be? Theres no legs for it to go between

I'm sure it works out somehow...

Nice! Your little brother's first lesbian!

Regardless, you never quit out of your internet. You left your porn on the living room comp. Then you passed out four feet from the chair with your hand still down your pants. We decided that we should go back to her place instead. Worlds best wingman.

Wtf he couldnt undo my bra, i asked him if it was his first time and he said 'with a girl? yeah'

Found the while-drunk-made folder i found on my laptop called 'definitely not porn'. 12 pics of chess pawns and prawn the shrimp things

My dad came in to wish me a happy birthday and found me passed out in my underwear with the lights on and a plate of meat on the bed. I bet he was proud to have contributed to my creation in that moment

>> Took him home. Told him i would rock his world. Passed out. A for effort f for follow thru

Not sure what happened last night, but there are four mini bikes outside and some guy is wearing my shirt passed out in the breakfast nook. Won't be telling the grand kids about this one.

>> She said I could do whatever I wanted to her. I pumped for 20 seconds, apologized, rolled over and passed out. I sit directly across from her at work. Awkward?

Please tell me I didn't pass out while we were having sex last night...and if so I am sooooo sorry.

Remember that time i ran away from the bar and passed out in a street cot?

Neither do i

Thats not how I planned it, its just the way she passed out

I just woke up without a shirt or bra on. Apparently I fell asleep with a quesadilla in my mouth. I can feel my liver hating me.

The ticket read 'Found nude in a tree'.

First off: I'm drunk so fuck you. Second: you weren't a bad girlfriend. Tres: thats 3 in spanish. Number 4: fuck 3 Doors Down

In the middle of sex he stopped to tell me that he loved me… then slapped my ass and told me ‘back to business’… im gonna marry him